Dadalectic

waking dream

Geena Matuson

Dadalectic

waking dream

First Edition, 2017

ISBN 978-0-9996162-0-8

geenamatuson.com | thegirlmirage.com

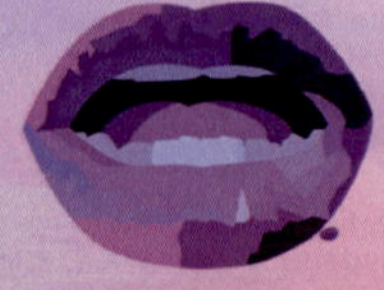

The Girl Mirage™

Contents

Introduction

I chose the title 'Dadalectic' with subtitle 'waking dream' as I believe it guides the reader towards a basic understanding of this text; I was both awake and asleep, the state of half-consciousness termed "hypnagogia" in which your mind may shut down but your imagination is not at rest. In this state, you are left with meaningful meaninglessness, a testament to dadaism.

I wrote this back in my mid- to late-teens, and in my mid-twenties created the art as I decided to publish this dada-esque, stream-of-consciousness collection of story-like poems and visions. Half the pieces in this collection (I call them "pieces" for I am truly unsure how to label them) were written as I was drifting in and out of attention in class, the other half written as I lay restless in a state of hypnagogia, trying to fall asleep but forced awake with images from my past. Some relate to real events – like the time I was almost constricted to death by a boa constrictor on a private (illegal) tour of the reptile room at a science museum when I was a child – and some relate to those visions we all have just as we're drifting to sleep.

While I have a passion for dadaism, I also appreciate structure and logical reasoning. Influenced by my studies in semiotics and my love of patterns, I structured this collection so that each piece connects from one to the other in ways that take a few glances to fully grasp. In a way, this collection functions as a story in itself, just like an ever-changing dream with one consistent mood or overarching theme.

I hope you enjoy my first published collection of works, and that you find something meaningfully meaningless as it relates to you. You can take this as seriously or as playfully as you'd like, and the next time you're drifting off to sleep, you can let your mind wander and discover what visions your imagination evokes. Perhaps you'll find a doll in a supermarket shopping for canned children, or perhaps a man wearing a knife on his head in order to cut the cake while his wife jokingly calls him "the most dangerous unicorn."

– *Geena Matuson, "The Girl Mirage"*

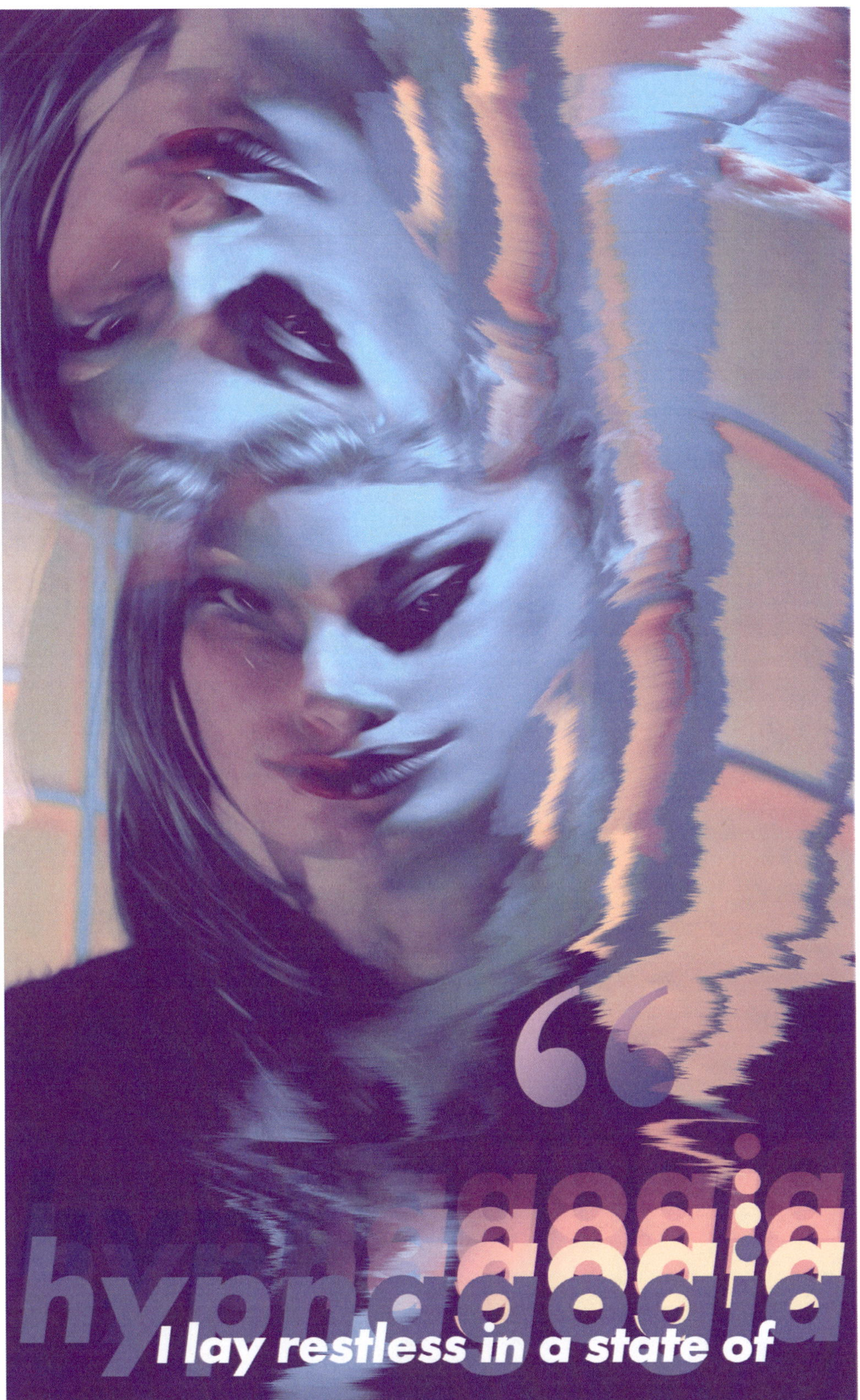
"
hypnagogia
I lay restless in a state of

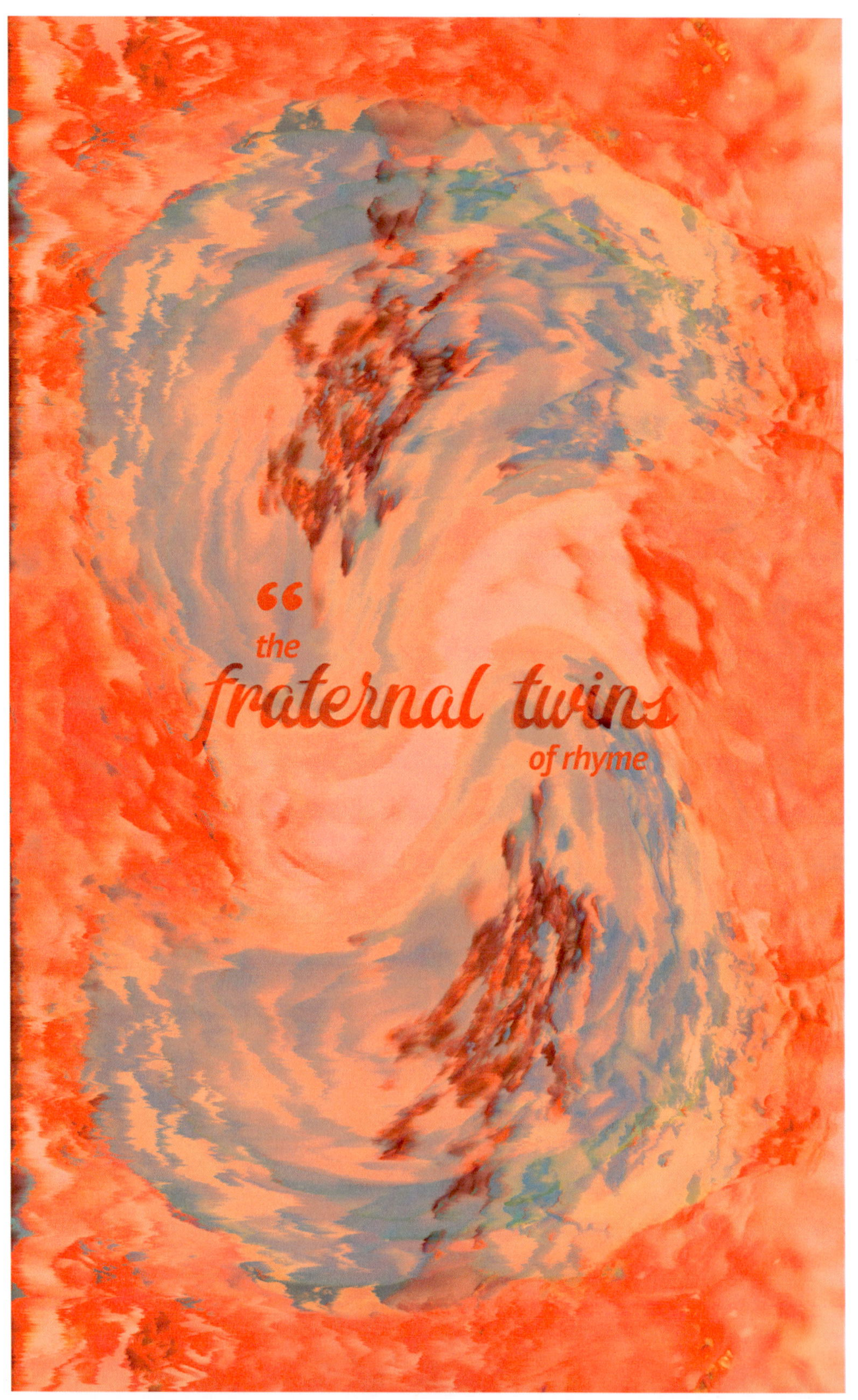
“
the
fraternal twins
of rhyme

A False Freedom

Chickens running free.
Consists, subsists, the life of me.

You flashback to a giant pile of sugar. Mining,
climbing to the top
to tumble through onto a bagel –

Neon. Blue neon and the grass beside you, near you.

On you, a cool whip. Wall sconces;
lighted sconces.

Blurred vision, jumping on a bed.
And here, here's an apple orchard. You watch yourself grabbing
for a caramel apple.
Tantrum – the trees are so fake, plastic and golden;
the styrofoam of diamonds.
Cold. A brisk chill, rocking, swaying back and forth.

Cake.

Elongated throat upheaval:
Rapid-fire, blitzkrieg potato guns, shooting chunks into a water bowl.
Flush.
Repeat.

He dropped the newspaper onto the coffee table. A slight breeze flips the pages and opens to news of a carnival. He decides it is a sign, and takes his Percival with him.

Independent, he likes to walk alone as a way to distract himself from attention – not to draw attention to himself – and Percival walks beside him, a very specific cat.

He sees her hair – distinctive hair. He approaches, taps her shoulder – but the man on stilts moves between them, friends pulling her away…

Smells of the Time

She sits so solemnly.
A different she, now.
          Not the girl who rhymes her thoughts,
                    not the girl who rhymes, at all.

She is in white.
Everyone else, in black.

You know, there is a reason for everything, and without knowing why everyone is dressed in black, this is all so strange. Further, to function without a reason why would be curious in that everything done would be so without reason.

I smell jasmine.
A cup of tea – but not here, no.
There.

She smelled like the 70s, and I told him as much.
He laughed, "Ah yes, you'd know because you weren't even *born yet.*"
"Well neither were you," I said, "so how do you know I'm wrong?"

A smell of must, of wood, of pot.
A comfortable, damp smell.

          You know, nothing rhymes with 'orange.'
          You could claim 'porridge,' a kind of imperfect rhyme.
          I suppose, as related to rhymes, two similar things are twins.
          Perhaps 'porridge' and 'orange' are the fraternal twins of rhyme.

    She sighed.

No one understands, just as no one understood,
or will ever stand to under the world.

Constricting

Picture it.
Science all around you.
Starry sky.

The star patterns change, highlighting the constellations. A woman's voice from above speaks of life and soothing music plays. The word 'Pleiades' is heard countless times. It is dark and warm – and very, very starry.

And now, you are taken to the reptile room.
You are young. You know, that age where you can fully function, but no one else realizes it yet. *That* sort of young.

And they lead you to that room – that room where the boa constrictor lives.

Yellow, smooth.
Full-grown, an adult.
You, a young child, holding an adult.

Smooth. Cold. Leathery, but slick; to say "snakeskin" might be redundant. But it is, as everything is redundant.

The weight overwhelms you – no one is helping. Why would anyone help?
And, so, it weighs you down.
And climbs on your neck. Creeps, more so.
And slithers and constricts.
Tighter and tighter.

Dizzy, the world closing in on you. Vision blurring, ticklish headache that
Sparks hit your eyes.
You cannot breathe.
Reach out. Do it. Reach out and grab for something. *Someone.*

But no one is there.
You stumble around.
Dizzy. Headache. Cold.
You cannot feel your hands.

Why is being cold an unpleasant thing to be? It is a feeling, like happiness.
A near emotion.

An adjective.

Restless

Restless she wandered, room to room.
In a fog these past few weeks, the sound of life muted.
She forgets things walking around, dazed.

Dazed, as though walking through a cloud.

She wandered back, eyes to the sky, to her room of animals. She always pats the leopard on the head; the taxidermist said he would never be the same again.

She wants to get out – and never come back.
To fly away and live in an orgy of sound.
Audible. Loud. The world of color.

She was locked. Her sanctuary, this room, was defiled by the one whose name did not go with her face.

She wandered.
A schedule to follow.
"You had us fired," the tight-faced
woman accused with a bony finger in her false face.
Her secretary, a balding man, aimed the gun at her.
She ran, but no one saw her.
She was hard to hear in an invisible fog.

She ran home on the bright pathway.
She couldn't stop.
She couldn't stop.

"What must it be like to be a tuna?"
No one eats tuna anymore.

She likes to vacuum – with the primitive carpet sweeper.
She likes to hear the crackle sound as she sucks up the pebbles. Little bits fall out as it goes, and so there is always more to vacuum, to clean, to distract.

Pronouns are her favorite tactic of confusion.

Why? You ask.
Why do you ask?

Haven't you ever wondered why people take children's teeth –
and give them money?

Why are you rewarding them for the loss of an appendage?

You know, she keeps her teeth in a little jar.
Over time, they smoothen, and crack down the center.
No one any longer keeps them alive.

'Let us watch rotting teeth' – that is the position of the parent. Careful, for they will steal your teeth. Next you know, they cut out your tongue, or at least wait for it to fall out when you ingest the rock, the poison, they slipped into your coffee.

Why do the elderly give coffee to the children?
          Stunters.
                    Growth is lost.

She could have been an inch taller, but they want you to remain short and retain your innate inferiority – and that is why they spit on your french fries.

Ah, do you see the little dots moving about the white walls?
          Or, rather, those dots are what comprise the walls.
                    Look closely; you will get an overwhelming feeling,
                              and you will see the wall move.
                                        Or. *Does it?*

Ah, now answer that: **if you do not see it, is it really there?**

N-Rays

I try, but I cannot.

To lay in the dark staring at the nothingness, hoping to pass into unconsciousness, is such a peculiar concept. Half the time I think my eyes are closed because it's so dark – but I soon realize I've "spaced out," so deep in thought that I was staring into the ceiling and didn't even notice.

A powerful mind's eye.

So strange, to lay in darkness and just…wait. Wait, for something to happen – to sleep. You wait, when you could be doing something productive until you cannot keep your eyes open.

In the light.

In the night.

Ironic that "light" and "night" should be so similar in English, and yet relate to two very different things, two different states. Or, maybe, that's just me.

"I cannot hold her in the dark; I cannot see her."
"If you can't see her, is it really there? Is anything really there?"

Is *she* there?

Is she there?

She's not there.

Oh wait, there she is.

No, that is an *N-Ray*.

Elusive, only seen out the corner of the eye. Look directly at it, and it's gone.

She is the light, she is the ephemeral night.

She is the milky white, just as she is the dilation.

She is the milky way, just as she is the dialectic.

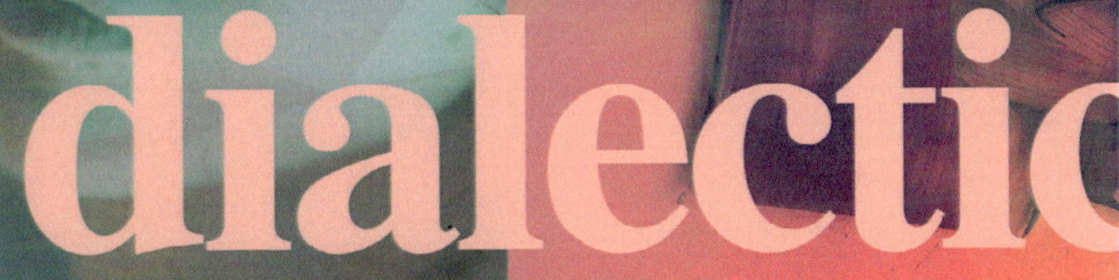

the art of investigating or discussing
the truth of opinions.

the **Hegelian** process of change in which a concept or its realization passes over into and is preserved and fulfilled by its opposite; also : the critical investigation of this process.

development through the stages of thesis, antithesis, and synthesis in accordance with the laws of dialectical materialism.

oxforddictionaries.com
merriam-webster.com

The Universe On Her Finger

Her hands, graceful, for she is graceful, but her hands make her arms, and her arms hold her body. Grace, a euphamistic mask for basic utility. And her hands, her hands are pale.

And she, too, is alone – just like you.
(Very alone.)

But lonely? She was but is no longer for, transfixed on her glowing red ring, she is comforted; the light emitted from the ring brings solace.

A sort of glassy, sort of crystalline red stone, a triangle amidst a
casing of silver. Within, the stone is fake – glass – a swirling
torrent of red and orange and burgundy. The texture seems
to be of the sand – of the islands.

Sand banks in the water – tiny, a bird's eye view through your eyes; a torrent.

She was mesmerized.

She could not grasp of this beauty, this tropologic gem.

Raw and gleaming.
Hot and beaming.
A universe on my finger.

I suppose I could let it linger.
Just a little longer,
As I sit and ponder the beauty within the glass…

But her thoughts were interrupted by a man –

Realize you are in a dark forest, and you're sitting upon the forest's ground. Brown, the earth. Mulch – *almost.*

Surrounded by tree trunks and, there (yes, *there*), you are sitting.

You can only see twenty feet in any direction; there are no openings in the trees. A private little niche, all with brown and red undertones.

Red.
Deep.

Incontrovertibly mesmerized, she thumbs the ring as a man
enters her secret home, her little section of the woods…

Flames

We met, and he knew me already. As I, him.
But neither of us remembered how.

He was not the brown-haired boy of years past, California.
The convertible, an incidental vacation.
No, none of that was him.

And I don't even remember his name.
Terrible.

We kissed, three times. Missed once, missed twice. Third time, close enough.
He was on TV, famous. A movie or show star, or something.

He hugged me – smothered, kisses on my neck – no, face.
    Lips. Lips only.
        Sweet. Tender.

He had his arms around me, and that can mean change.
That warmth felt, the feeling of being wanted for once.
        Unappreciation leads to inner death.
    Just kill to get it over with.
So many men are killers, and they don't even know it.

Mental.
    Emotional.
        "Theocratical."

He laughed at my jokes and said, "This is why I love you."
    We held hands, and he held me.

Mosquito, a woman, watched us.
    From my window shades, up above.
        Both of them, Calypso and Belize.
    (At this point, we shall give the bugs a name.)

I have always been rather fond of Calypso…

Like a Coward

He grabbed her and pulled her in, doing what he'd wanted to do since he first laid eyes on her.

He gave into impulses – but that never stopped.

And, so, he stood there, daydreaming in
the fleeting of thought as he stared in silence.
She, just smiling.

It is a tragedy. "A tragedy and a travesty," he said, in order to show that two similar words are very dissimilar in meaning, forcing the listener to question their inaccurate denotations.

She pondered and asked, "are they not the same?"

But this, too, was in her head, for she was too embarrassed, and so she only smiled a phony, knowing smile.

When you find someone to be the Bonnie to your Clyde and they say, "I would do that with you, too," – is that bad?

Well what about you, is it bad you would do that, too?

So, what are you waiting for?

Coward.

You would rather run away than live, they say, in an attempt to cover your cowardice. But, then, if you are Bonnie and Clyde,
aren't you also running away to hide?

So, how do you ever know you're living?

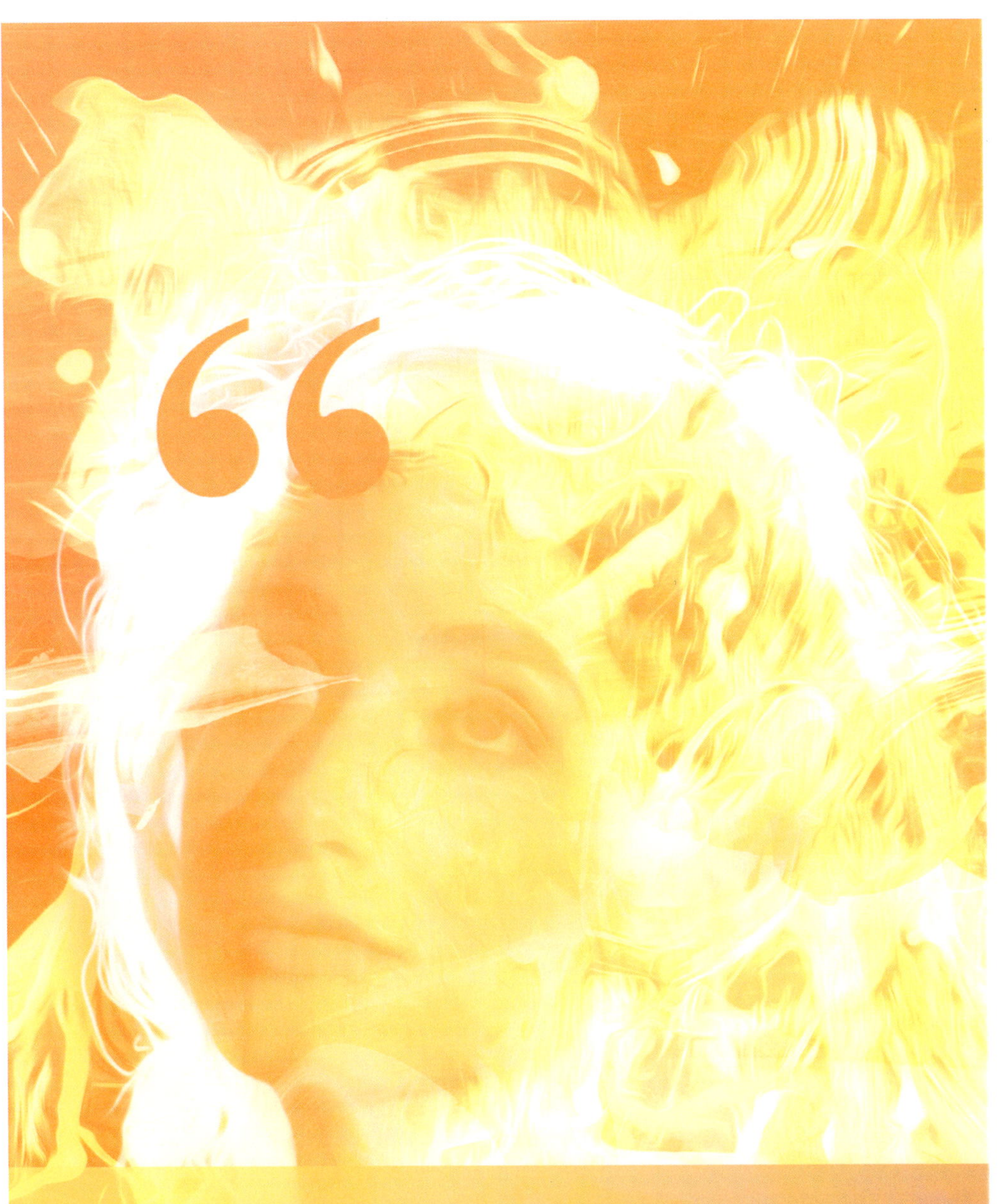

My, how we set the city ablaze in the wheat field haze; our robotic bodies combusted.

My, how we burn.

The Running Train

Why is it the doubtful, live?

As if you were a train that was deteriorating before your eyes,
and you do not believe it.
No, you deny.
Doubt?
No.

You cannot accept it.
You do not accept it.
It is just that; your mindbox is so simple,
to comprehend such a thing is beyond you.

The man who is a schizophrenic, the man who likes himself.
He likes the soap.
He is on that train,
on the train with you.

Shiny and golden
long, full of body
soft and smooth.

The hair of the girl in front of you.

Rings are slimy,
like his.
Bright, flaming.
Heated discussion.
Divorce.
A cycle. A circle.
A ring.

Does it descend in a slanting manner?
J ump ahead?
And where it has begun,
and begun where it ends?

Does it even have an end?
Do you see it?
(No.)

As the man on the train discovers, everything comes to an end;
you only see it as a chain for as long as the end is distant.

In a hammock.
Picture it.
In a hammock.
Hot. Not at all cold.
Maybe warm, as opposed to hot. Tepid, if we're being specific.
If you were a lizard, I suppose you'd be comfortable, really.

You are watching yourself look at him.
You swing in and out, back and forth;
closer and further from yourself.
No, not the you in the hammock –
The you in the hammock is gently rocking.

The you *watching* you – *you* are swaying back and forth. You cannot control it and, through your eyes, you get closer and further, all the while swinging. And it is hanging over a rubbish heap. The walls are lined with old cans, license plates and hubcaps, tin garbage covers.

Now it is dark, and people are disappearing.
The house of cheap pine wood is slowly…
Crashing?

Not audibly, though, and so – you missed it. Sections fall off into oblivion, but you do not see it, as you are concentrating on the you in the hammock, wondering if there's a chance you'll swing further and further, and never swing back.

And you are on a train, the train speeding on a track parallel to an oncoming in the opposite direction. And it is brisk out today, very brisk, as is swimming in a bath of tea.

Ice-T.

But not nearly as cold as ice connotates frozing to be.
And the train seems to be on the left side – heading forward –
in the UK they would be on the correct side of the road.
But here, you are in the wrong.

Track.

Outside In

The car smells of seltzer.
Cherry seltzer.
A fizzy atmosphere.

Maybe it'll bring back old memories, or remind you of that dream about a Persian rug company…

Piles miles high: Persian rugs.

On the highway: all of the orange leaves on the road, all of the yellow leaves on the pavement, all of the green leaves on the trees.

Just riding, riding past all the trees.

The clouds are striped – pointing North. Clouds that look like sandbars in the sky…

I watched the clouds overtake the sky, from a fractured ribcage to an expanding, smoke-filled lung overrun with asthma traveling across the atmosphere, engulfing the cerulean with a cancerous plague. These clouds do not esch across the sky, but glide across so seamlessly that the blue does not know what is coming – as it is engulfed.

Soon, the sky will be white without a trace of blue.
Would anyone know the sky was once blue?
Would they even believe it?

No, just as I wouldn't believe that the sky was, once, red.

Will there be clouds?

What color would the clouds be?

Pink

You look like pink, like opals and firecrackers, like words describing translucence the eye cannot capture alone, but can only know exists in theory.

You are the median, the time, the nothing – the everything.

You are the white and the black, just as the black was, once – white.

Don't look now.

Don't think now.

Don't – *now*.

"Well don't look now!"

But you did.

A flash in the pan – and the nothingness disappears.

You wonder why no one asks for you to be there, just tells you the all after, tells you they had fun with their friends while keeping you separate. It keeps you there, alone, where you've been your whole life.

"Why are you separate?"
"You're like a secret – a 'secret friend.'"

"You are a secret. A thing; not even a person, but a dehumanized abstract idea or concept, a nothing-of-any-consequence."

"An afterthought, really – you are, don't you know that?"

Barely a thought, a fraction of a second.

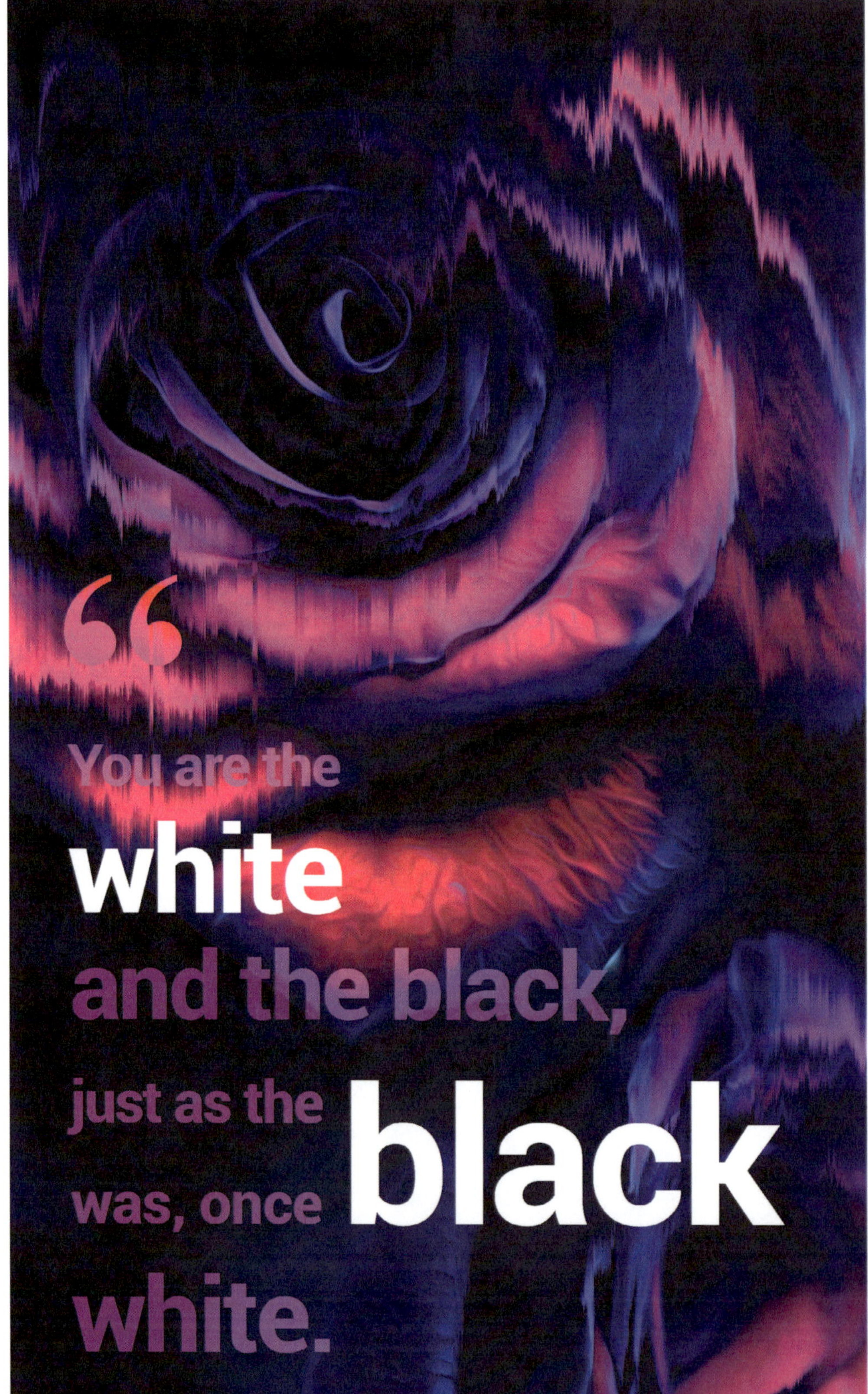
"
You are the
white
and the black,
just as the
black
was, once
white.

You and Time Do Not Exist

She often misunderstands time.

If you do not exist, how can time exist around you?

Is it that you do not exist, or that you do not want to?

You so fear time – time, the one thing you cannot control – that you choose to pretend it does not exist.

But how can that be, if *you* exist?

This is why you choose to be nonexistent; if you do not exist, time cannot exist – time cannot control you if you do not exist within its realm.

Yet, isn't time's control forcing you to change, to become nonexistent? Do you not see that by being – or, rather, by the absence of being – you are allowing time to control you, still?

Would you rather be – or, rather, not be – nonexistent,
than remain in existence, giving time the upper hand?

We are all submissive to time.

There is only one way to escape time's control; it requires you to change just one more time – and then, not at all.

Fall Asleep

She reached for her tea, convinced that would quiet her mind; falling off to sleep was really no easy trip.

What I would give to be insane.
She thought. *Why, I might even give my sanity.*
Her grasp loosening on the teacup, she collapsed.

Asleep.

She often wondered how one sleeps without feeling tired, and concluded that only people who have the propensity to be bored could ever grasp such a concept.

Calypso was never bored.
More so restless than anything.

The thumping drums do nothing to soothe her mind. In conclusion, she hadn't really fallen asleep. (Tricking one's own mind doesn't work, apparently.)

At the shoe store, the man sizing her foot confessed his life story. After learning of his wife's pregnancy at fourteen, having been sixteen at the time, she commended him, "I am, might I say, quite honored to have met you."

He seemed puzzled.

"You did not run out, but took up the respectable job of the shoe salesman to support your young family. I commend you."

She was given the shoes for free.

WHY?

She gazed up at the ceiling.

What the light looks like now is a stack of individual papers floating in space about to fall into a neat stack – but froze just before they could land. It looks like a row of tapestries – flags – hanging from the ceiling of a castle at an angle. It looks like butcher knives – large ceiling blades – poised to fall on my body.

What the light looks like is me, somewhere else. Somewhere not here.
Away.
Disappear.

Sometimes when I just wake up, that first open eye, I am disoriented.

I feel I'm in my first house, the house from when I was six. Or, sometimes, the house in which my mother now resides. But never the yellow house with the slanted bedroom ceiling.

Never the yellow house.

The house in which all my scary stories took place, had always pictured them. A death house, a secret body buried in the rectangular shaft in the attic, the swarm of flies in the light bulb – my bedroom.

The house of decay.

It felt like the house I read about in the book grandma gave me in that same house, all those years ago. Everyone thought the old woman was a witch who could walk through walls, but the door, it turns out, blended into the wall and, so, she was not a witch, at all.

I always felt like people came and went in our house, the yellow house, in the night.

And I find myself listening to all the ones that scare me most.

Maudlin's Marmalade-Laden Nipples

There is no sleep for the dead. There is no time for the dead – we must take their dreams and harvest them, stand in a line, a circle, and photograph their graves, marking the sin of the zombie's hand, marking the apex of the world's greatest disappointments.

There is no time for the rain to fall and to behead Maudlin's precious bee; rolling it in marmalade will do no good now.

Take your life in your hands.
Take your life.
Take your life.

Fuck the feeling of camaraderie felt with a friend, on the golf course, the free coconut drinks and the napkin rings reminiscent of the marker.
Take the time, take the death.
There is no time in death.

Watch Maudlin's bee, her marmalade-laden nipples, so sweetly falling atop your grave, marking the end of days.

We must abolish it. We must take a stand against the widow of time, of death – of existence.

"I feel like the indigestible byproduct of sexual apples and rancid plums, fornicating atop a mound of fruitcake," she said.

Her sweet marmalade thighs full of lust fall open, but you find disease in the form of bees and they spread their promises of lost time, photographing the herds of consumerism at its worst.

We must abolish it.
We must abolish it.
We must abolish it.

Carnivorous beasts of the hungry demon.

I do not prevent myself from further ingestion due to the impending odor arising from the thought of future comestibles.

The Smart Sheep

You don't know what it feels like.
You don't *know* what it *feels* like.

As if my mind is melting into tears behind my eyelids, dancing in colorful sights and false smiles dripping into sarcasm and hatred deep in my throat.

If there were no people – things – this place, I would not worry. I would not worry about anything. If I could go away to a place where no place could be placed…

Nowhere.
Nowhere is that place.
That placeless place.

I wouldn't even keep a calendar. Or perhaps I would – just to track the years. Maybe. I'm not sure. No; I may not even have a calendar.

"But what about your friends?"

No, I would be completely alone.

"But, wouldn't you tell your friends?"

No, I would just…sort of…disappear.

It's like that game you play in gym class, the sheep and the wolf. The lights go off and all the other kids – "sheep" – hide within the thick blue. The trick, they tell you, is to remain in one place. If you move around, the wolves can find you. Remain in one place, and no one will ever know you're there. Well, I will be the smart sheep, and disappear without a word, remain Nowhere and never be found.

"It sounds like you want to kill yourself."

Are you mad? (What the fuck?)

I would go out into the woods in the middle of the night, and hear sounds.

The sounds get closer and closer.

Is that leaves, rustling? Are these sounds…shapes?

And I am eaten alive.

The Evergreens

Above the evergreens.

Fields, off the side of the road.
Appear with machines standing around,
Made of wood and shaped like humans –

No eyes are seen; they can see with their minds, implanted in them like grass. There are two of them, but there may be more to come. They walk around, searching for the other.

I walk by with my parasol.
They turn to me with their lasers aimed,
Sucking me into their wooden land –

The city appears in the distance.
So many dark things moves about.
We all battle for the rule –

Of the wheat field in which we inhabit.

So many dark things moves about.
The morning sky is red, orange – blue.
An arc of stones appear –

I stand in place of a fallen one, this creature.

I see the rollercoaster go overhead; the little girl lost her crown. I enter the potato's lair to retrieve the golden orb, the place made of stone unlike the norm. The attic door was bolted shut, but I knew the combination lock.

A splinter drove into my wooden knee, bringing me back.
Back to the bad man.
The man I loved –

Yet, my clone did not.

She helped the prince, whom she loved.
Adorned with flowers, they greeted each other,
Shy and bashful while I watched from afar –

The bad man walked into her trap, and I couldn't say a thing to stop his boat as I watched from a distance; closed-circuit television.

He sailed to the frosty sea while my clone remembered my past…

The yellow house with the white picket fence,
The flower boxes lining the sidewalk.
The prissy neighborhood girl –

A thin, blonde eight-year-old.

She walked down the lane and dug-up the garden.

While I yelled and turned into another, I handed the boy a pail of slime and headed towards the future. He smiled like a cartoon character in love, at my clone never to know love like that of his I was, trapped between soup and the bad man's demise.

No one knew I loved him.
He reached for the chicken fingers.
And slid down the ice.

So lovely out, so very lovely and white.

Snow, dancing through the trees, watching him hit one with his body.

And I watched that lone tree.

The evergreen tree.

My maker.

My city syndrome.

My, how we set the city ablaze in the wheat field haze; our robotic bodies combusted. We were ahead of our time – ahead of our science.

My downfall.

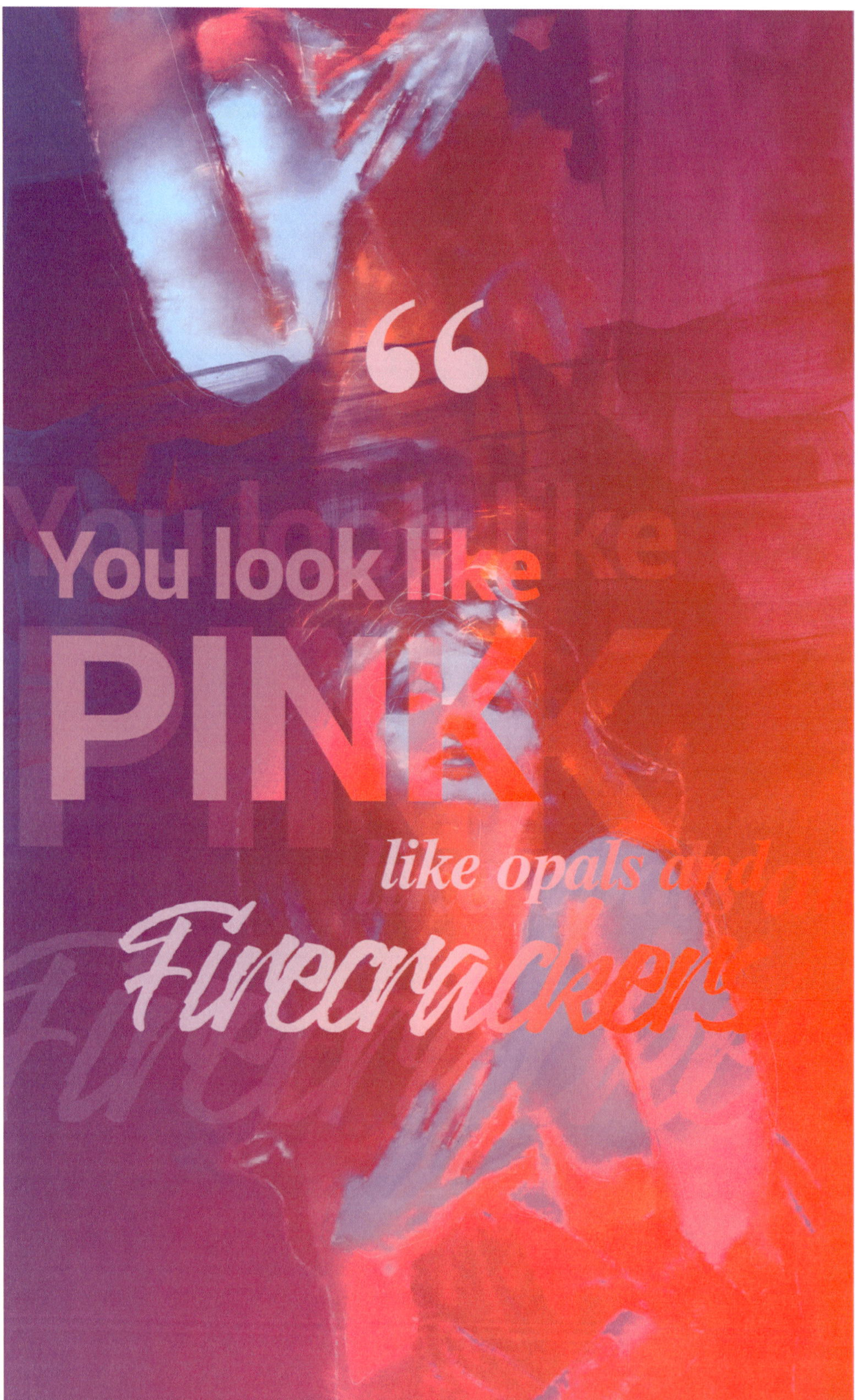
"
You look like
PINK
like opals and
Firecrackers

My, How We Burn

Like the flame burning on the round, it is untorchable.
Fallen and melting; the flame burns invisible.
No one can see the flame growing.

The rare seer who can recognize the flame, can touch the flame, can feel its burn.
Can feel its desire to warm.
Can touch it –

And then, they are gone.

The candle's flame burns again.

Alone.

My, how we burn.

A waxy exterior
Only hides; feigns
A façade of –

Flames.

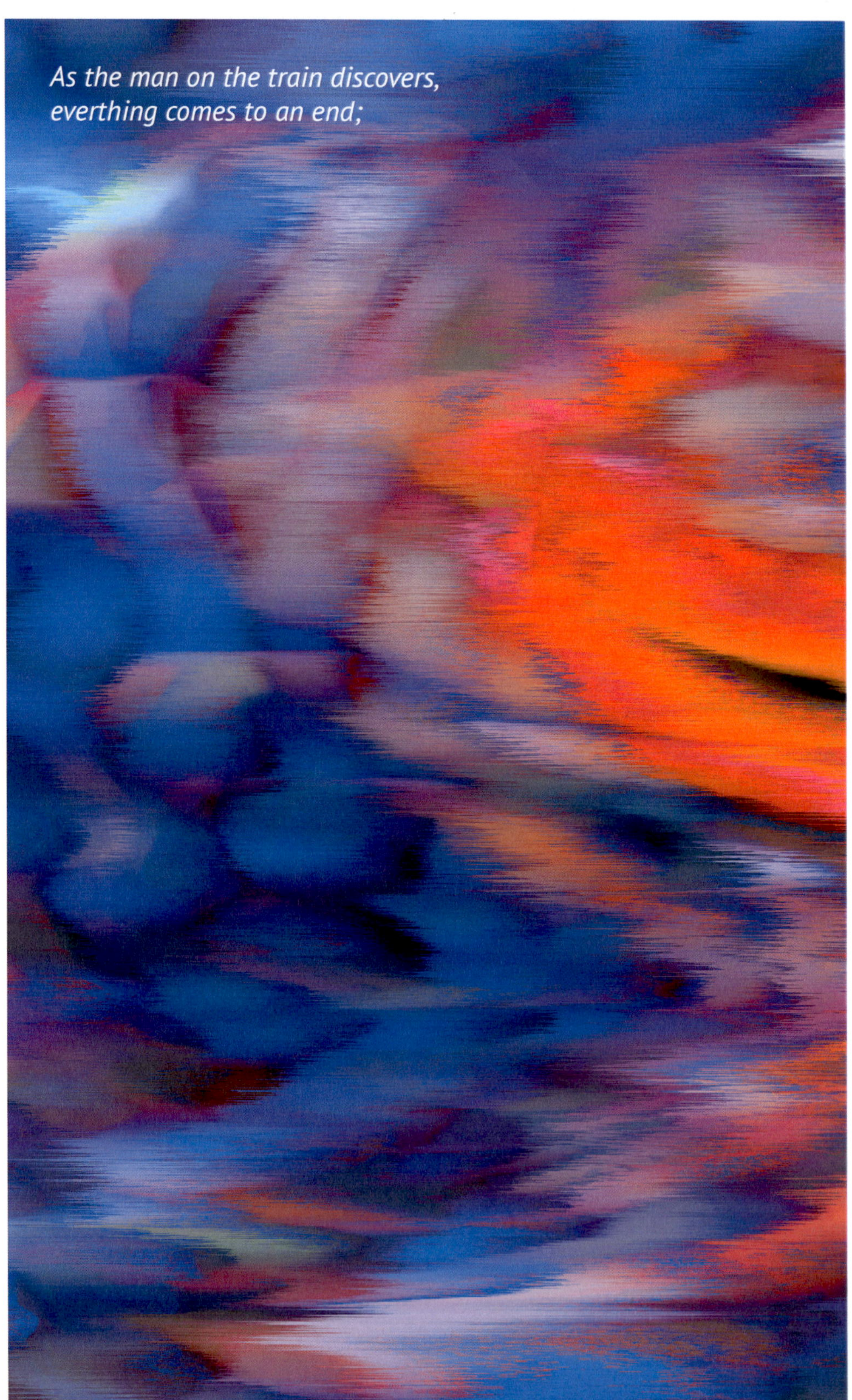
As the man on the train discovers,
everthing comes to an end;

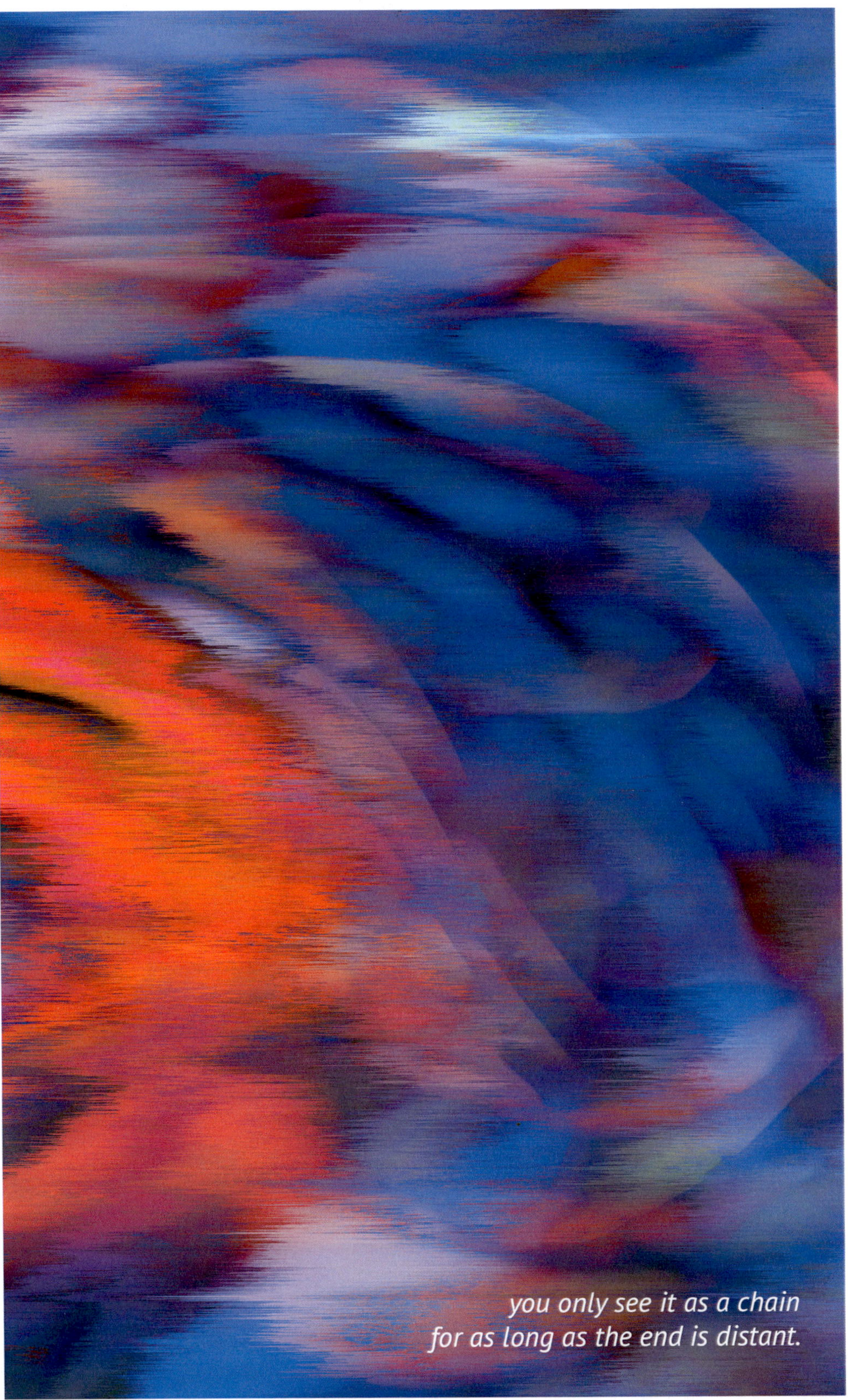
you only see it as a chain
for as long as the end is distant.

Dadalectic

waking dream

Geena Matuson

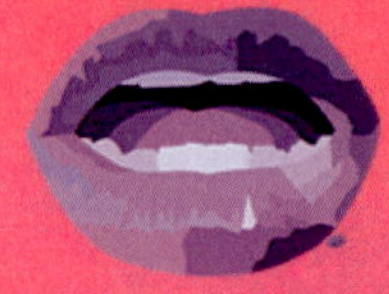

The Girl Mirage™

The Author

Geena Matuson is The Girl Mirage™, award-winning Multimedia Director and Digital Producer telling stories through the strange and surreal, written and spoken word, and visual arts. Interested in semiotics and psychology, her work often evokes a sense of synaesthesia, and even a sense of humor.

In 2013, Geena graduated from Massachusetts College of Art & Design with a BFA in Film/Video. Her expansive works have been featured in festivals and gallery shows internationally including CyberArts Festival, Architecture Boston Expo, and PH21 Gallery in Budapest.

Currently, Geena sits on the Board of Trustees with Medfield Memorial Public Library where she advocates for STEAM education and programs. Additionally, she is pursuing advanced degrees in arts journalism and digital marketing, while also printing and publishing her "strange and surreal" works.

You can shop and subscribe for news, updates and discounts for products online at **www.thegirlmirage.com**.

www.ingramcontent.com/pod-product-compliance
Lightning Source LLC
LaVergne TN
LVRC092209110826
845154LV00023B/155

* 9 7 8 0 9 9 9 6 1 6 2 0 8 *